FIND A TREE
IN A NUTSHELL

From Dreamers to Doers

Also Written by Daniel Armstrong

How to Live Your Dreams
Find a Tree and Get Started

Live Your Dreams Now
Read About It! Write About It! And Do Something!

Unlock Students' Potential
The Blueprint for Transforming America's Schools

Free South Africa
The Columbia University Divestment Movement:
A Personal Perspective

FIND A TREE

IS AN EMPOWERMENT PROGRAM THAT
INSPIRES YOUTH AND ADULTS TO ACT WITH
URGENCY AND CONFIDENCE IN PURSUING
THEIR DREAMS TODAY.

FIND A TREE®

A Pathway to Your Dreams®

BACKGROUND

Daniel Armstrong worked in Ghana, West Africa, for two years, pursuing business and development projects. While there, he also worked with Ghanaian youth, coaching basketball and teaching them how to launch their own businesses. Two of those youths, twin brothers Jonas and Jonathan Atingbui, dreamed of having a school of their own. However, they had no building or other resources. Armstrong advised them to "find a tree and start their school there." Soon, Jonas and Jonathan had nearly 100 students coming to their school under a tree. Seeing their success, a businessman in the community gave Jonas and Jonathan a new building he had constructed to use as their school. That is how the Find A Tree program got its name and its inspiration.

INTRODUCTION

I BELIEVE...

YOU can have an exciting, fulfilling life...
YOU have untapped talents and unrealized dreams...
YOU can make a difference in the world...
YOU can live your dream...
YOU have to find a tree and get started—today...
NOW is the best time to get started on your dream.

Find A Tree provides a new point of view—yes, you can live your dream if you start today doing what you can, where you are, with what you have. Dreams are not for the distant future, flights of fantasy, or just for the young. Dreams are for the brave, those who dare to disregard their own doubts, as well as those who would tell them "no, it can't be done." Dreams are for those who are prepared to fail, fall down, and get back up and try again. Dreams are for those who refuse to settle for the ordinary and believe they must try, regardless of the outcome. Dreams require more than sincere hoping and wishing. Dreams are nurtured with knowledge and action. The Find A Tree Principles contain strategies and psychological tools for turning dreams into reality. This booklet will provide the reader an introduction to the nineteen Find A Tree Principles.

I hope this booklet inspires you to take the steps to live your dream and experience a whole new world—the world of your dreams.

—Daniel Armstrong
Los Angeles, California

The Find A Tree Principles

1. **Identify What You Are Passionate About—Your Interests, Talents, and Gifts**

   Know yourself, and then you can be yourself.

2. **Determine Your Dream: Find a Tree and Get Started**

   Act now where you are, with what you have.

3. **Explore Life**

   No path of action is a mistake. Learn and move forward.

4. **Nurture Your Dream with Knowledge**

   Living your dream starts by getting knowledge.
   Read about your dream today.

5. **Empower Yourself**

   To live your dream, you must find a way to produce results, not excuses.

6. **Be Willing to March into Hell**

   If you can withstand the test of fire, you will be stronger, wiser, and shine like pure gold.

7. **Build the Trust of Others**

   Your character matters.

8. **Embrace Struggle**

   The pathway to your dream is never easy.

9. **Sometimes You Just Have to Have Faith**

   Great things only happen when fueled by great faith

10. **Create Opportunities through Service**

    Give before you get.

The Find A Tree Principles

11. Value People

Treat all people like VIPs.

12. Plan, Prioritize, and Manage Your Time

Use your time like money; invest it wisely.

13. Distinguish Yourself with Excellence

Always give your best effort to be amazing.

14. Understand the Process: From a Seed to a Tree

Dreams can take time. Be patient.

15. Tap Into Your Creative Genius

Be creative and bold. Your dream may depend on it.

16. You Will Achieve What You Expect and Try For

Problems have a way of working themselves out when faced with a determined opponent.

17. Lead Yourself

Dream of a better world, then find a tree and get started. The world is waiting on you.

18. Start a Business

Start a business by focusing on what you have, not what you lack. Many have done it. You can too.

19. Work in Harmony with Universal Law (There Is No Santa Claus)

Find a tree and get started. No one is going to bring you your dream.

Identify What You Are Passionate About— Your Interests, Talents, and Gifts

Know Yourself, And Then You Can Be Yourself.

What makes you happy? What brings you fulfillment and a sense of purpose? Life would be so exciting if one day I could _____." What is that for you? What makes your soul sing? What is important to you?

Make a list of twenty of your talents (activities that come naturally to you) and your interests (things that catch your attention, even if you are not good at them or likely to do them). This list can be any combination of talents and/or interests. Study yourself until you can list a total of twenty. If you get stuck, start with the simple: "I like good food... I like a good movie...."

Making this list is the starting point to living your dream. You must first know yourself. Knowing yourself is the starting point for determining what to study in college, or even whether you should go to college, what career to pursue, how to spend your free time, or what to do in retirement.

Determine Your Dream:
Find A Tree and Get Started

Act now where you are,
with what you have.

A dream is like a seed planted in your mind. You must first plant a seed in order for something to grow. Define what you want. "I want to be happy" or "I want to be successful" is too vague. What makes you happy? Define clearly what you want. Draw a picture of you doing that activity, so you can see yourself doing what makes you happy or doing what you would like to do in order to be successful.

A dream does not have to be a job or career, but it can be. A dream is something you want to be, do, have, or experience in life. There is a difference between a goal and a dream. A goal is something you can reasonably expect to accomplish if you put forth the effort. A dream is big. If you tell friends or family members your dream and they think you are crazy, then you know it's a dream.

Once you have defined and determined your dream, hoping and wishing it will come true will not work. You must do something. The starting point could be getting knowledge about the area of your interest. Go online or to the library and start by reading about the topic of your dream. Create a project that embodies your dream. Do something related to your dream. For example, if your dream is to one day have your own restaurant, let your friends know you are available to cook for their next party. Who knows, someone attending the affair may love your food and want to invest in your future restaurant. For good things to happen, you first must find a tree (identify the resources at your immediate disposal) and get started...doing something...today!

3

LEARN · ACT · ENGAGE · MOTIVATE · INSPIRE · EXCEL · ACHIEVE · TRANSFORM · DREAM ·

Explore Life

No path of action is a mistake.
Learn and move forward.

People often tell me their dream is to have a dream. Many do not know their dream. Determining your dream, like finding your purpose in life, may be a journey of self-discovery and reflection. If you are struggling to figure out what your dream could be, you must become proactive in exploring your interests. If there was a banquet table full of different types of food, some foods you may recognize and others you may not. To know which foods you would like to have you would probably want to have small samples.

After sampling, you should know if you like a certain dish or not. Use the same approach with your dream. Lay out all of your interests and potential dreams and sample them by exploring them. This may entail going online and reading about the area of your interest. Sometimes after just a few minutes of reading, you may recognize that a certain dream is not for you. Move on. If something catches your imagination, keep reading and then talk to others with experience in this area.

Continue to explore and take action on your dream; eventually your heart will tell you whether a dream is for you or not. Start exploring today until you can determine a dream that is right for you.

Nurture Your Dream with Knowledge

Living your dream starts by getting knowledge.
Read about your dream today.

Going after a dream with no knowledge is like looking for
something in a large, pitch black room with no windows or
light. You will probably bump into things and have a hard time
trying to find what you are looking for. Knowledge is the
mental light you will need to see the pathway to your dream.
The first step toward realizing your dream is to get knowledge
about your dream. If your dream is to travel somewhere in the
world, start by exploring the travel and housing options and
their costs. Read about the history, culture, and people of your
intended destination. If you dream of having a certain career,
research the necessary training and education requirements.
If you want to work on a social issue, find out what is currently
being done on that issue and what organizations are active in
your community.

Empower Yourself

To live your dream, you must find a way to produce results, not excuses.

Champions in sports often credit hard work, determination, and teamwork for their success. Champions rarely make excuses or complain about referees' bad calls. To live your dream, you must accept responsibility and overcome all obstacles and opposition. Blaming others will not enable you to live your dream. What can you do today to move forward on your dream? Do that. Focus on what you can do to move forward with your current resources. Be proactive and productive, every day. No one can tell you "no" if you look to yourself and no one else to make your dream happen. This is the Find A Tree approach to empowerment. Overcoming opposition or obstacles will ultimately make you stronger. If you stay focused on what you can do today, in time your dream will begin to take shape.

LEARN · ACT · ENGAGE · MOTIVATE · INSPIRE · EXCEL · ACHIEVE · TRANSFORM · DREAM

Be Willing to March into Hell

If you can withstand the test of fire, you will be stronger, wiser, and shine like pure gold.

Going after your dream is not always easy. If it were, everyone would go after their dreams. Pursuing your dream will often be hard. Be prepared for a difficult challenge. Gold is found in ore and is separated from the ore after going through hot fire. This fire purifies the ore, and what remains is pure gold. You may be required to go through the fire of many challenges before achieving your dream. This test of fire will prepare you, if you can stand the heat. In these challenges will be valuable lessons that you need in order to live your dream. Some lessons you will have to learn through the test of fire. You will not learn them in a classroom or from reading a book. Sometimes, if you want to live your dream, you will be severely tested. This test of fire may separate you from your dream and cause you to lose hope and quit, or it will make you stronger and better prepared.

7

LEARN · ACT · ENGAGE · MOTIVATE · INSPIRE · EXCEL · ACHIEVE · TRANSFORM · DREAM ·

Build the Trust of Others
Your character matters.

Keep your word.

Sometimes we intend to keep our word. For example, we plan to return a book to a friend or repay a few dollars to a co-worker, but we forget. Develop a system to remember these promises. The oft-repeated excuse--"I forgot"--does not build the trust of others in you. When you keep your word, people know they can rely upon you. Once people know that you keep your word, even for small things, then they are more likely to trust you and refer you to others who can help you with your dream and share with you opportunities that may benefit you. When your word is your bond, then your credit card can be your word. This is particularly useful when cash is short.

8

LEARN · ACT · ENGAGE · MOTIVATE · INSPIRE · EXCEL · ACHIEVE · TRANSFORM · DREAM ·

Embrace Struggle

The pathway to your dream is never easy.

A dream should be something difficult to achieve. If your dream can be easily achieved, then I would describe it as more of a goal. A "struggle" is defined as "a long effort to do, achieve, or deal with something that is difficult," according to the Merriam-Webster dictionary. A dream is a struggle. When we struggle to achieve something great, we increase our understanding and build our character. Going after a dream is like climbing a great mountain. You will fall. You will feel fatigued. However, if you can get to the top, you will grow in self-confidence knowing you endured to the end. You must develop the character of someone who can fall down and keep climbing. Belief in yourself is needed to achieve your dream. Never run from the difficulty of pursuing your dream; accept the challenge and overcome.

9

LEARN · ACT · ENGAGE · MOTIVATE · INSPIRE · EXCEL · ACHIEVE · TRANSFORM · DREAM

Sometimes You Just Have to Have Faith

*Great things only happen when
fueled by great faith.*

Going after a dream often does not make logical sense. The odds of your dream happening may be small, but still you have to believe. Some will tell you that you are wasting your time, your education, or your future, but still you have to believe. Your dream may never come true, but you must always believe you will succeed.

Create Opportunities Through Service

Give before you get.

Demonstrating what you can do by using your talent to help others can open doors of opportunity to you. If you offer to do volunteer work in the area of your dream, you are less likely to hear "no." Once people can see you demonstrate your talent, then others are more likely bring opportunities and resources your way. We have all heard the expression "time is money," but take time to help someone using your talent and help may come your way in return (and you will feel good about yourself as well).

ACT·ENGAGE·MOTIVATE·INSPIRE·EXCEL·ACHIEVE·TRANSFORM·DREAM·LEARN·

Value People

Treat all people like VIPs.

Effective people skills are some of the most valuable skills to have. When people like you, they are more likely to want to help you, buy from you, and support you. Make it a practice to show courtesy, respect, humility, and kindness to all people. Dr. La-Doris McClaney, who happens to be African-American, owns high-rise commercial buildings in Beverly Hills, California. She would visit her buildings disguised as a member of the janitorial staff. Dr. McClaney got a clear picture of her tenants' character by how they treated her in her cleaning lady disguise. Listening, avoid criticizing, and respecting others are habits that will cause doors and hearts to open to you. The most difficult people can be turned into allies when handled with effective human relations skills. Whether a person is a secretary to someone whom you would like to meet or a person who reports to you at work, people are more likely to want to help you achieve your objectives if you treat them well.

Plan, Prioritize, and Manage Your Time

Use your time like money; invest it wisely.

Whenever I hear people say, "I didn't have time" (unless the person is a mother), I usually know they do not manage their time very well. Even a busy mother can arrange her time to accomplish her dream. She may just have to allocate fifteen minutes a week to accomplish it. The process may take a while, but even a busy mother can pursue her dream.

After attaining knowledge about your dream, write a plan of action to move forward on your dream. The initial phase may be a project that involves using your talents related to your dream. Decide what you want to accomplish over the next thirty, sixty, and ninety days. Create specific objectives so you will be able to determine whether you accomplished your goals. What do you want to have completed over the next week, tomorrow, today?

Your plan should have specific tasks to be completed and a date you intend to complete each task. These tasks are the stepping stones to your dream.

With a specific list of tasks written down, you are no longer just dreaming. You now have a blueprint to build your dream into a reality. Prioritize your time to allocate time to your dream. Study your use of your time. If you are spending hours on social media and watching TV, then you have time to work on your dream. You will need to make your dream a priority and adjust how you allocate your time in order to have time to complete the tasks in your plan of action.

Based on your plan of action, identify priorities for the week that you must accomplish in order to make progress on your dream. Next, make a list of daily priorities for each day of the week. In order to get the daily priorities accomplished, create a time management plan the night before.

Here is an example:

6:00	Wake up	5:00	Workday ends
6:20	Shower and dress	5:30	Dry cleaners
7:00	Breakfast	6:30	Home – Rest – Dinner
7:30	Drive to work	8:30	Read about your dream
9:00	Start workday	9:00	Return phone calls
12:00	Lunch	10:00	Bed

Read about your dream for 15 minutes prior to starting work

Effective time management will ensure you have the time to get all your tasks done and remain relaxed knowing you simply have to follow your time management plan.

13

Distinguish Yourself with Excellence

Always give your best effort to be outstanding.

Excellence is making sure every detail is right. Excellence is making something better than the rest. While many will settle for what is "good enough," commit yourself to make excellence your habit and you will stand out. As Oprah Winfrey says, "People notice excellence."

14

Understand the Process:
From a Seed to a Tree

Dreams can take time. Be patient.

Dreams are not microwaveable. Most dreams do not get completed fast like popping a frozen dinner into the microwave. Dreams often take time to take root, sprout, and grow—ever so slowly. While we want our dreams to happen quickly, and others may expect us to quit when they do not happen as soon as we would like, there are valuable lessons to learn at each stage of development and progress. Like a tree that needs sunlight and water to grow, nurture your dream with knowledge and action and it will grow and bear fruit in time.

15

LEARN · ACT · ENGAGE · MOTIVATE · INSPIRE · EXCEL · ACHIEVE · TRANSFORM · DREAM ·

Tap into Your Creative Genius

Be creative and bold.
Your dream may depend on it.

Obstacles will appear when going after your dream. You must not allow an obstacle to stop you. Be creative and find solutions. Sometimes you may have to reach out to a powerful person, use humor to side step someone trying to deter you, or simply have a lot of chutzpah—shameless audacity. When faced with being stopped by an obstacle, you must decide: how badly do I want my dream?

16

You Will Achieve What You Expect and Try For

Problems have a way of working themselves out when faced with a determined opponent.

Many times we kill our own dreams with our negative thoughts. If a basketball player thought, "I am going to miss this shot," most likely he or she will miss. On the other hand, if you see a commercial on television advertising a chocolate shake and you think, "I sure would like to have that chocolate shake," most likely it would not be long before that shake is in your hand. Eliminate the thoughts that will stop you from working on your dream—"I may fail,"... "What will people think?"... "I don't have the money." Instead focus on the tasks of your plan of action and overcome obstacles as they present themselves. Focus on your immediate goals and not the reasons why your dream will not work.

17

Lead Yourself

*Dream of a better world, then find a tree and get started.
The world is waiting on you.*

Waiting on others to bring you what you want often only leads to disappointment. If you see a problem in your school, community, or company, think of what you can do to make it better. Create a plan that depends on you making it happen, even if that means rallying the support of others. Leaders must first have a vision and then attract people and the resources to make their vision a reality. Leadership, whether it's as a school principal, a corporate CEO, or mayor, is never easy. People rarely jump to implement a leader's vision, so do not get frustrated when people do not jump at the chance to follow your lead. However, with persistence and a creative strategy, you can make a difference.

Start a Business

Start a business by focusing on what you have, not what you lack. Many have done it. You can too.

To be in business means to make something, do something and/or sell something and receive money or something of value in exchange. Within most people's list of talents is a potential business. I happen to enjoy cleaning and in college I started a carpet cleaning business—The Dirt Patrol. We fought grime, not crime. Starting a business does not mean you must quit your job or necessarily require a lot of money. Start small. The multimillion dollar company, The Famous Amos Chocolate Chip Cookie, began with Wally "Famous" Amos baking cookies at home and giving them to friends as gifts. Later, when people heard about his cookies and wanted some, he began selling them and his company was born. Many great ventures started small---in a garage or dorm room. Google and Facebook are examples. Use your garage as your office and factory as Steve Jobs and Steve Wozniak did to create Apple.

Examine your list of talents ("Identify What You are Passionate About—Your Interests, Talents, and Gifts").

What talent do you have that can benefit others? Start in service to others ("Create Opportunities through Service").

If your service or product is valuable, ("Distinguish Yourself with Excellence") word will spread and prospective customers will contact you asking to hire you or pay for your product. Treat your customers like VIPs ("Value People") and keep your promises to your customers ("Build the Trust of Others"). While building a business will be challenging ("Embrace Struggle"), always be on time ("Plan, Prioritize, and Mange Your Time") and your customers will continue to

Work in Harmony with Universal Law (There is No Santa Claus)

The magic will happen and you will enter a whole new world once you find a tree and get started on your dream.

Santa is not going to bring you your dream. You must get up and do something. Once you get in motion, then good things in the form of resources, people, and opportunities can come your way. Do not worry about what you do not have, focus on what you do have and figure out a way to do something today.

How to Live Your Dreams
Find a Tree and Get Started

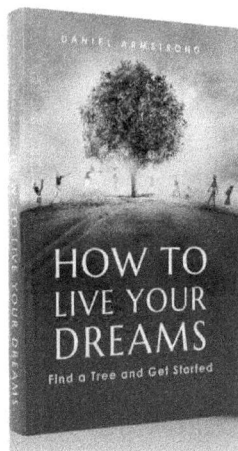

- A Practical Blueprint
- Personal and Professional Growth
- Lessons that Jump Off the Page
- Spark Real Life Change
- Thoughtful Exercises
- A Powerful Journey of Self-Discovery
- Step-by-Step Model for Self-Improvement

For a complete explanation of the Find A Tree Principles and the corresponding workbook.

Live Your Dreams Now
Read About It! Write About It! and Do Something!

- A Practical Blueprint
- Personal and Professional Growth
- Lessons that Jump Off the Page
- Spark Real Life Change
- Thoughtful Exercises
- A Powerful Journey of Self-Discovery
- Step-by-Step Model for Self-Improvement

Provide youth readers 10 to 14 years old a pathway to their dreams.

About the Author

Daniel Armstrong is The Dream Mentor, an author and motivational speaker. He's widely recognized for his work within the American education system–providing empowerment programs to educators, administrators and students through his Find A Tree program.

Daniel's mission is to inspire and mentor, both youth and adults, to pursue and actualize their dreams. Daniel Armstrong earned his Bachelor of Arts degree in Political Science from Columbia University in New York City. At Columbia, Armstrong was the founding chairman of the Coalition for a Free South Africa, an organization whose four-year campaign resulted in Columbia divesting from corporations operating in apartheid South Africa. Armstrong earned his Master's degree in Business Administration and Juris Doctorate both from UCLA. He is also a Ford Foundation Fellow, having studied youth development in Zimbabwe, where he organized a national tour by the Harlem Magicians, an American basketball team. The tour's opening night game was the largest multi-racial gathering, at that point, in Zimbabwe's then brief history, following twenty years of civil war.

For more information on Daniel Armstrong and his Find A Tree program, visit www.danielarmstrong.com.